A REFUGE FROM THE STORM

AN INTRODUCTORY GUIDE TO STORM SHELTERS AND SAFE ROOMS

SHAWN CLAY

TABLE OF CONTENTS

This introductory guide is designed to assist you, the reader, in learning about the various forms of storm shelters and safe rooms. All information contained is provided as reference material only. Please consult a dealer or expert in the field before purchasing or installing a storm shelter or safe room in your home or other building. This will ensure that all structural necessities are met, as well as local building codes, permitting, inspections, etc. As with most things in life, there is no such thing as a "one size fits all" answer to what kind of shelter is best for you. This guide is designed to get you thinking about all the factors that need to be taken into consideration for your specific situation. Once all those factors are addressed, then you can make a more informed decision about which type of shelter will best serve your family's needs.

INTRODUCTION

The Dalai Lama was once quoted as saying, "Even when a person has all of life's comforts - good food, good shelter, a companion - he or she can still become unhappy when encountering a tragic situation."

His words are true, but really need to be taken a step or two further in order to matter to us. This book is all about taking the notion of shelter a step further. This guide isn't just about life's comforts. It's about survival, self-reliance, and prepping for anything the world might throw at us.

I think the Dalai Lama's quote rings better for our purposes with a slight revision:

When encountering a tragic situation that can make one unhappy, a person should always be prepared with life's comforts - good food, good shelter, and a companion.

This guide will help you with shelter. Good food and a great companion are up to you.

Myself, and the author, Shawn Clay, are no strangers to the necessity of a strong and durable shelter in times of need. I grew up in a hurricane-prone coastal area where usually, from one to a half dozen times a year, we were forced to evacuate or hunker down as winds blew trees around and houses disappeared into the surf. Even after that, I worked as a member of a U.S. Department of Homeland Security disaster team that chased natural disasters all over the United States. Clay is an unfortunate friend to a different kind of storm, having lived for years in one of the most tornado-prone areas in the southeast United States.

We understand more than many that shelter is vastly different than other needs. Sure, you should prepare for anything, but some things require more time. If you need food, clothing, or weapons, you can find them or scavenge them somehow. If you need a durable shelter, it needs to be planned and built. This takes time, and it may not be time you have. We have seen bad things happen and people caught unaware and unprepared. Please don't let that happen to you.

It is our hope that immediately after reading this guide that you'll find yourself out in the yard stepping off measurements for your new shelter or even heading to the nearest home improvement store to buy supplies. If you're not, you might need to reconsider your priorities.

– Dr. David Powers

Dr. David Powers is an adventurer, philosopher, and pioneer. He is considered an expert in team building and goal-setting, and having perfected these skills in life-threatening situations, now teaches them in conferences and other settings. He is a best-selling author in cognitive psychology and experimental education. He is a decorated member of the Marine Corps and a founding member of the U.S. Department of Homeland Security. He is married and the proud father of three feral boys and one princess that he and his wife homeschool. His mission in life is to find the magical best mug of coffee in the world. Be sure to check him out at CallSignRedbeard.com.

CHAPTER ONE

What is a storm shelter/safe room and why do I need one?

I would wager to say that most people have seen a storm shelter at some point in their lives. Those living in the rural south and the great plains of the Midwest know that there are certain times of the year that they are more likely to be used than others. If you've ever driven through those regions, you've likely seen shelters dug into the sides of hills or buried in the yard within a short distance of a house. This is out of necessity, since a tornado or straight-line winds can be on top of a community with little to no warning sometimes.

So, what does this have to do with you? Maybe you've gone your whole life without considering one. Maybe you've dodged a few close calls and figure that luck is on your side. I've lived in the south all my life, where springtime often brings tornado watches and warnings, and have unfortunately come into close proximity with tornados twice during those years. Needless to say, both were certainly eye-opening experiences. The sheer power and devastation that these storms can bring is something that only can be described as incredible. One can look at the news footage, or witness firsthand, the total destruction that these storms leave in their wake. Many, many lives have been lost over the years to these events, yet many have also been saved due to the presence or availability of a shelter to take cover in. The purpose of this guide is to outline the various forms of shelters and safe rooms, in order to provide a better understanding of their function and intent, and to outline the need for every family to have some sort of plan in the event that a catastrophic storm is bearing down on them.

The terms "storm shelter" and "safe room" may seem very similar, but each actually has an intended purpose. The storm shelter is a room or enclosure that is specifically built to withstand the force and devastation that a large tornado will unleash on everything in its path. It is designed to keep the occupants protected until the storm is over and it is safe to come out. While a safe room can also provide this level of storm protection, its intended purpose is to provide the occupants of a home or business with a secure location to gather in should a dangerous situation arise, such as a home invasion or active shooter, and you need to seek secure shelter.

Storm shelters are typically designed from either concrete or steel and most manufacturers have them rated to withstand a certain level of impact from an approved source, such as the Federal Emergency Management Agency. Storm shelters can be built into a home during initial construction, such as digging a storm cellar or reinforcing a bottom floor room, or the homeowner can opt for installing a prefab shelter during the building process. However, just because your home did not come with a storm shelter, there are a myriad of makes, models, and manufacturers that can ensure one is able to be added to your existing home. It should be noted early on that while a basement that is located all or partially underground is advantageous, it is not a guarantee that it will withstand a strong tornado or hurricane. Unless the ceiling and walls of the basement are reinforced, the structural integrity of the home may be compromised during the storm and collapse onto the occupants seeking shelter in the basement. For years, there was an old wives' tale that the southwest corner of the basement was the safest corner to be in during a tornado. This false assumption likely comes from the mistaken belief that most tornadoes approach from the southwest, and that any debris they generate would fall into the northeast corner of a basement. History has proven this myth dangerously false many times over the years, as entire houses have collapsed into the basement during a tornado passing through. A properly-designed and purpose-built storm shelter that is accessible to all the occupants of the home is the best defense against these powerful acts of nature.

Safe rooms, on the other hand, may be a room in a house or business that has a reinforced door preventing entry to the room. Some models have reinforced walls as well. Sometimes referred to as a "panic room", models are available that can withstand gunfire and have all manner of technology such as closed circuit TV cameras and separate phone lines should the intruders decide to cut the main house or business line. These types of rooms are often seen in areas of the world, such as Israel and some of its neighbors, where bombings and rocket attacks are frequent. Most houses in these areas have an interior safe room designed to protect the occupants from these attacks and the resulting shrapnel.

Now that we have a cursory understanding of the difference in a storm shelter and a safe room, let's examine the different types of shelters and rooms available. The goal of this guide is to help you select the right option for your family or business's needs.

CHAPTER TWO

What size shelter do I need?

One of the first considerations when deciding on a shelter design or model is to know exactly how much room you are going to need inside. FEMA addresses this issue in their guide on storm shelters (a link is provided in the appendix) with the following statement.

FEMA guidelines for number of occupants per shelter are as follows: For a tornado shelter - 5 square feet of space per person. For a hurricane - 10 square feet per person, because you will probably be in the shelter longer. Wheelchair users require 10 square feet per person.

As you can see, a storm shelter is not designed to be luxurious, only to provide a safe place to ride out a storm. Some shelters allow adequate room to stand and move around, while others are designed for the occupants to be sitting or even kneeling. The size of your shelter will be determined by how many people you plan to bring in and the physical location that your shelter will be placed in.

When considering how large of a shelter you need, consider not only your immediate household, but possibly neighbors as well. While it's up to each household to develop their own contingency plans, what will you do if you have people begging for help at the last minute? My shelter is designed so that my family of four can easily stand or sit in it, but does have enough space where we could accommodate our elderly neighbor or the family on our other side. It would be cramped, but considering that our main threat is a tornado, the duration of being confined will likely be limited to the few minutes that the storm is raging around us. Admittedly, there is the chance of debris blocking the door, but that is of little concern as long as we survive the storm. A cell phone is part of the kit that will be present whenever we enter the shelter, so help will hopefully only be a phone call away once the storm has passed.

In addition to people, don't forget about your pets. We have two beagles and a cat, so they will be there with us as well. It won't be an optimal setup, but we will survive nonetheless.

Another factor to consider in selter size is the physical condition of the occupants. As the FEMA statement mentions, wheelchair-bound people will take up double the floor space, a consideration if you have elderly family members. I personally keep four of the folding camp chairs in my shelter so that my family can sit if they choose. If you have people with limiting physical characteristics, you want to ensure that your shelter is roomy enough and accessible enough for them.

Finally, think about what this storm shelter represents. It's a place to go and escape a terrible weather event. However, it can also serve as a vault for your sentimental or heirloom items. Now, I'm not suggesting that you try and install a shelter that's the size of an Olympic swimming pool, but you could mentally catalog what items in your possession would be irreplaceable in the event of a tornado and consider being able to store them in your shelter before a storm comes. For example, I have my gun safe in the back corner of mine. It's anchored into the concrete with 8 inch lag bolts secured into concrete anchors. It allows me to not only keep my firearms safe and secure 24/7/365, it also allows me a place to put our cameras, laptops, photos, phones, etc. in the event a storm is coming. Use your own judgement, as "stuff" is often replaceable, but think about being able to store those "must keep" items in the shelter. We make a practice of moving our "must keeps" into the shelter whenever a storm looks likely in our area. It only takes a few minutes and it's worth doing just for the peace of mind it brings.

Safe rooms, on the other hand, can be as roomy or spacious as your imagination and budget will allow. I've seen examples that resemble the interior of a five star hotel, complete with sitting areas, sleeping areas, restrooms, entertainment hubs, etc. However, I would wager to say the average family that is installing one of these rooms for the purposes of surviving a home invasion would likely have one with a more utilitarian look, as the purpose is simply to survive the ordeal unharmed. If it were me, I'd rather spend my budget on armored walls and a vault door instead of leather sofas and a wet bar.

Your individual or family circumstances will decide what type of room you want to build. If you are in a high crime area, a safe room may be the most logical room to build. If you're in tornado alley, it's a no-brainer that the storm shelter is the way to go. Or, you could do a room that is a combination of both and kill two birds with one stone.

The typical shelter will cost between $2000 and $9000. The wide range takes into account the myriad of options available for the owner. This may seem like a large investment to make, but just as I discuss in my guide to generators, this is an investment not only in your family's safety, it can also add value to your existing home. Some homeowners opt to run electricity into their shelter as well, to power lighting or electronics when not in use during a storm. As I mentioned above, they can be utilized for storage, but NEVER allow them to become just another overstuffed closet, as there is little to no time available to move everything out should a storm show up on your doorstep. Some states have a program through their Emergency Management Agency that will allow grants or tax incentives for the purchase and installation of a shelter. Info about this topic can be found in the appendix.

CHAPTER THREE
Above-ground Shelters

This type of storm shelter is your typical box-style room that can be pre-fabricated and self-installed, assembled on site, or delivered complete and installed on site. These shelters are usually constructed of either rebar-reinforced concrete or hardened steel. Sizes can range from single-person models to community-style models that are placed in areas such as mobile home communities or church and government buildings.

As with all major purchases, please perform your due diligence when selecting a storm shelter. Different door setups, steel and concrete thickness levels, and installation procedures vary from vendor to vendor. At a minimum, ensure that the shelter carries a Fujita scale rating from a reputable testing lab, such as Texas Tech. This rating should specify the level of storm that the shelter is capable of withstanding. Since tornados can launch trees and other debris at your shelter at speeds well over 100 miles per hour, you don't want to spend your hard earned money to find that your shelter fails at the very moment you need it the most.

Placement for these shelters is entirely up to the buyer. Some homeowners prefer to purchase one and have it installed just outside the home, usually in a backyard or patio area. In some communities with homeowner associations, shelters can be constructed to match the existing home. In other areas with less restrictive zoning, a simple concrete room may be chosen to sit right behind the house, offering the occupants a quick exit from the main residence into the shelter.

My personal storm shelter came from the good folks at Fain Storm Shelters, out of Jackson, TN (http://fainstormshelters.com). The people there are great to work with and have info on financing programs as well. Shown here is my personal steel shelter that I selected for my home. It is located in the back corner of my garage, and provides easy access for my family in the event of a tornado. Assembly was around four hours with my contractor and one assistant following the detailed instructions included with the shelter. The shelter arrived via semi-truck on a pallet with all the necessary hardware. As noted in the instructions, the shelter panels and door can be configured in a variety of ways, giving the homeowner options regarding entry method. As you can see, my cat has the utmost confidence in it.

If a concrete shelter is more along the lines of what you are looking for, they manufacture this type as well. Sizes range from small to community size. Like most storm shelter dealers, Fain Storm Shelters can deliver and install your shelter, usually in as little as a single day. I consider my shelter to be the best investment I've made in my home.

Since my particular shelter was the type that anchors into the existing concrete pad of my garage, I opted to take carpet tiles and line the floor in order to provide a little more comfort and padding should my family and pets have to hole up in it for the duration of a storm. The size of my shelter is six feet wide by nine feet deep and I opted to locate it in the back right corner of my garage. This way, I can still pull our vehicles into the garage to protect them from hail damage during a storm, yet still have easy access to my shelter should the storm spawn a tornado. I spent many hours researching what would work best for my family and our home before purchasing this shelter, and I would advise anyone considering a shelter to do the same. What works for me may not necessarily work for you.

CHAPTER FOUR

In-ground Shelters

In-ground shelters are designed to keep the occupants safely underground while the storm passes over. The concept has been in use since mankind huddled in caves to escape the elements. Various militaries and governments utilize these types of shelters to shield their complex communication hubs and weapons storage depots. Whether it's the NORAD facility inside Cheyenne Mountain in Colorado Springs, Colorado, or the FEMA command center at Mount Weather near Bluemont, Virginia, underground shelters serve as fallback locations for the nation's military and civilian leadership. These types of facilities are designed to withstand both conventional and nuclear weapon strikes.

As with the above-ground shelters, sizes range from cramped to roomy, with as many available options as your mind can conjure up. Common options are benches or fold-out seating, emergency jack (for opening a door lodged by debris), and battery-operated lighting. Some shelters are available with custom sleeping quarters, televisions, air conditioning and heating options, air filtration, and closed-circuit security monitors to keep an eye on what's going on outside. The options available range from practical to extravagant, and are only limited by the size of your budget.

The majority of these shelters are designed for use outdoors, and can be found constructed out of reinforced concrete or fiberglass resin and steel. Since the intent is for the majority of the shelter to be shielded by the earth, the door and frame will be the most heavily reinforced areas on this type of shelter. They can be located in the ground near the house, or they can be buried in a hillside if your local terrain is conducive.

In addition to the in-ground shelters designed for outdoor placement, there are also some designs that lend themselves to in-home usage. Shelters, such as the ones shown on the following page, are constructed so that they fit into the garage floor, therefore allowing ease of access to the shelter along with the added benefit of not taking up too much usable floor space. The next time you go to an instant oil change, take a good look at the pits that you park your car over. This design allows the workers to be able to access the undercarriage of your car without having to have hydraulic lifts, etc. This is virtually the same concept as the in-ground garage storm shelter.

This type of shelter has a few slight drawbacks as well. For instance, since this underground shelter is designed to be used inside the home, there is a good chance that if the house collapses during the storm, the door will be blocked. As you can imagine, that will essentially trap the occupants until debris removal crews arrive. To mitigate that threat, many dealers of this type of shelter will also provide your address and, in some cases, GPS coordinates to local emergency management agencies so that help will be able to make its way to you quicker once the storm has passed. However, as with any type of shelter, a cell phone is an essential tool to have, along with a jack to open a door blocked by debris. An EPIRB (the same type of emergency beacon that most boaters carry on their vessels) would be a good investment as well, as it would broadcast a distress signal to rescuers.

Another point to consider when using this type of garage shelter is its proximity to the home's hot water heater. Since most hot water heaters are located in the garage, it's easy to see how the combination could become a problem very quickly. Should a storm blow over the water heater, there is a potential that the contents will flow over and into the shelter, showering the occupants with hot water. While this is certainly preferable to being caught outside in a storm, it can still add to the terror for some family members, especially children. Should you decide to purchase a shelter of this type, please take this possibility into consideration.

CHAPTER FIVE
In-home Safe Rooms

Sometimes referred to as "panic rooms", this type of shelter is designed to be located in a central area of the home in order to allow quick retreat into it by the occupants in the event of a home invasion or other serious threat. The room is designed primarily to keep people out, often being constructed in a similar fashion as a bank vault. Some versions are available with bulletproof walls, floors, and ceilings.

Often times, these rooms are designed to be "hidden in plain sight." As an additional layer of security, the entrances to these shelters are often designed as a bookcase or other structure to ensure the anonymity of what lies behind, as seen in the picture above. I had a friend growing up whose father constructed one of these rooms in his basement. There was a false cabinet that swung out of the way, revealing his "man cave", where all of his firearms and reloading equipment were kept. Only those who knew that the room existed could tell that the cabinet was false, as it even had functioning doors and he kept various automotive and hardware items inside it to give the appearance that it was nothing out of the ordinary. At the age of 13, I thought it was undoubtedly the most amazing thing I'd ever seen.

Since these rooms are designed to be used when time is of the essence, often times a digital or thumbprint scanner is used to open the door to the room, although some of the more basic models have a standard doorknob to access the room, and several reinforced locking bolts on the inside of the door to secure it to the door frame once the occupants are inside.

As with some of the various types of storm shelters, these rooms also can perform double duty as home vaults for valuable or heirloom items. Costs on these safe rooms can vary all over the spectrum, depending on one's budget and requirements. These types of rooms are best installed during initial construction of a home, but retrofitting an existing closet or spare room is also an option if you have a finished home or move into an older home.

As with storm shelters, it's a good idea to have a cell phone present in your safe room. This way, even if you have a landline that gets cut prior to the home invasion, you have a way of accessing law enforcement and getting help on the way as soon as possible. And while safe rooms sometimes tend to conjure up images of hidden bunkers inside a mansion that only the elite can afford, the fact is that any closet or unused room in a house can be turned into a safe room for a relatively minor cost. For instance, most interior doors in modern houses are hollow-core, meaning that they are simply wood or thin metal sheeting over a hollow frame, they can be less than reliable when trying to keep out a determined intruder. The solution would be to purchase a security door that is solid core and that has a metal frame that can be anchored into the doorway. Add in a few heavy duty bolt locks on the interior side of the door (such as at the top, middle, and bottom) and you will be in a much more secure position if the home invaders try to break the door down by brute force. Granted, solid core doors on all the exterior doors of your home will also help slow down or prevent an intrusion, allowing you a few extra seconds to make it to your safe room and take up a defensive position while alerting the authorities.

CHAPTER SIX
Location, Location, Location!

The actual location of your storm shelter or safe room is one of the most important factors to consider before you purchase or begin construction on one. For instance, if you decide to go with an outside shelter that is in-ground, do you know where the utility and sewer lines are in your yard? Does your yard slope in such a way that water may seep in during a heavy downpour? If contemplating an above-ground shelter, is the hillside you have chosen as a location comprised mostly of clay or is it granite and limestone that will have to be chiseled or blasted away? Does your county or neighborhood have any restrictions that dictate the size of an exterior building in regards to property lines? Is the ground that you intend to place your shelter on strong enough to bear the weight without sinking or settling, or will you need to pour a concrete pad for it to sit on? How far is it from your house, and can you safely get your family in it during wind, lightning, hail, etc.?

In regards to shelters inside the home, such as garage shelters, will you be able to access it in a hurry, and not be blocked by vehicles or all the storage totes containing your holiday decorations? If your choice is the in-ground garage shelter, will your hot water heater pose a threat if tipped over or punctured by debris? Are you located in a remote area that may take rescuers some time to respond to?

If you are planning on an in-home safe room, will it be accessible by all members of your family? Is it located on a floor that would prohibit someone with limited mobility from accessing? If utilizing a digital electronic lock, does it have a battery backup or manual opening options should the power to it fail?

As you can see, selecting and installing a storm shelter or safe room is not something that you just point and say "put it there". Time and consideration must be taken to ensure that it is installed safely and correctly. As I've mentioned previously, in-home shelters are most easily installed during initial construction, but a quality contractor can renovate most any home to accommodate most any type of shelter. If you are planning to build, I strongly encourage you to consult the FEMA manual referenced in the appendix. There are many schematics and drawings for various types of storm shelters that you could utilize for your own. Take advantage of all available resources to ensure that your storm shelter or safe room is the right fit for your situation and your family. Your very lives may depend on it. Also, research your state's emergency management agency's website. There are many states that offer incentives in the form of tax breaks or grants to residents who purchase or build a storm shelter. You can find a link to the FEMA funding guidelines in the appendix and resource guide at the back of this book.

Since we are in the subject of location, this would be a good time to check your weather radio status. If you have one, is it located in a central location where an alert will be heard and noticed by the occupants of the home? Have you checked the batteries in it and is it properly set up to notify you of the threats to your immediate vicinity? While most cell phones have the option to notify the user of impending severe weather, it is important to have a dedicated weather radio in your home as a backup. Most weather radios pull watches and warnings straight from the government NOAA offices and are the most reliable when it comes to keeping apprised of an incoming severe weather event. I keep my personal radio set to begin flashing upon receipt of a warning or watch for my county. The location of your storm shelter will be of little benefit if you aren't warned enough in advance of an approaching storm, such as a middle of the night supercell that pops up suddenly with little or no warning. Good quality radios from companies like Midland are available for less than $75 and are a great investment for your home. If your residence is more than one level, I would strongly advocate for having one weather radio per level for maximum effectiveness.

CHAPTER SEVEN

Items to keep in your storm shelter or safe room

If you have decided that a storm shelter or safe room is necessary for your home or business, there are a few items that should be kept in it at all times. Depending on how many people you plan on occupying it will dictate the size and quantity of your shelter supplies. When it comes time to purchase items, or you are considering buying in bulk to supplement your other preps, check and see if your state or city has a sales tax holiday for emergency preparedness items. A lot of states in the southeast will have a holiday like this (usually in September, since it's severe weather awareness month) where sales tax is waived on all emergency and disaster preparedness items.

Most people in the prepping community may choose to keep a "bug out" bag with all kinds of survival essentials in their shelter. At a bare minimum, I would suggest the following:

- Bottled water

- Emergency food (granola bars, beef jerky, etc.)

- Flashlights with extra batteries

- Emergency radio with hand crank charging capability

- Whistle / Air Horn (to signal for rescue)

- Blankets

- Cell phone

- First Aid kit

If you are in a coastal part of the country where hurricanes are an annual occurrence, I would suggest adding a few items for comfort, since the duration of the storm will be much longer than a tornado. Items to entertain children, battery-powered lighting, folding chairs or cots, and even a small chemical toilet may be necessary additions to your emergency supplies. If you have a child or family member who is prone to anxiety attacks that are triggered by storms, you may want to consider noise-cancelling headphones as well.

If an interior safe room is your goal, you may want to consider similar items, as well as some sort of method of self-defense. Depending on your skill level, this may range from pepper sprays or impact weapons up to a firearm of some sort. This weapon (or weapons) would be used as a last resort should the safe room somehow be breached by an intruder. Check into your local laws and regulations regarding allowable weaponry and justifiable deployment. If you are planning on incorporating a firearm into your plans, then please get training on the proper storage, use, and handling of your particular weapon.

Only you and your family can determine which type of shelter is best for your situation. I encourage you to talk about it and discuss together what your greatest danger might be and where the most accessible locations might be. If you have young children, the whole concept of a storm shelter or safe room may lead to fear at the onset as they sometimes assume that since you are taking precautions, something must be about to happen. My son was very traumatized by the outbreak of tornadoes that swept through our region in northwest Georgia in April of 2011. At the time, I did not have a storm shelter, so we made a shelter for ourselves in the small closet underneath our stairs. It was the strongest part of our home, since we do not have a basement. After seeing firsthand the devastation and power that these storms bring with them and how they literally ripped homes away from their foundations, I could readily see the error in my thinking.

When I decided to install a shelter, my son was very nervous at first, because of the memories it brought back to life. Fortunately, once it was installed and he got to go in it and see how strong it was, he was actually relieved and on board. For parents, taking care of our children is the most important task we have in this life. If you do not have a storm shelter and live in a part of the country where strong tornadoes or hurricanes are a fact of life, I would urge you to strongly consider installing a shelter. We spend money every day on items that have little or no practical value. How much better off would we be to apply some of those funds to protecting our most precious of assets?

In closing, I thank you for purchasing this introductory guide to storm shelters and safe rooms. I sincerely hope that you found it useful and thought-provoking, and that it spurs you to begin to take stock of your own family's emergency plans and that if, Heaven forbid, you ever find yourself in the path of one of these deadly storms or experience a home invasion, that you and your family have a safe place to shelter and seek security in during that time. Please check out the resource section for additional information and checklists to use when selecting what shelter is right for your situation. If you have questions, I would strongly encourage you to speak to a licensed contractor or storm shelter / safe room dealer to find out the particulars that would apply to your situation. Always remember that material things are replaceable. Your family is not. Choose wisely.

APPENDIX/RESOURCE GUIDE

This section will provide additional information on storm shelters, safe rooms, dealers, installers, and other related accessories and information.

STATE SPECIFIC STORM SHELTER DEALERS

(While some states do not have specific dealers, many of the nationwide dealers will be able to service them.)

ALABAMA

Valley Storm Shelters
Huntsville, Alabama
https://valleystormshelters.com/

Lake Martin Storm Shelters
Alexander City, Alabama
https://www.lakemartinstormshelters.com/

ARKANSAS

Arkansas Storm Shelters
Russellville, Arkansas
https://arkansasstormshelter.com/

Shelter Solutions of Arkansas
Little Rock, Arkansas
https://www.sheltersolutionsar.com/

CALIFORNIA

Atlas Survival Shelters
Montebello, California
https://www.atlassurvivalshelters.com/

FLORIDA

Florida Storm Shelter
Windermere, Florida
https://www.floridastormshelter.com/

Storm Shelter Depot
Southport, Florida
http://www.stormshelterdepot.com/

GEORGIA

Survive-a-Storm Shelters
Thomasville, Georgia
https://survive-a-storm.com/

FamilySAFE Storm Shelters
Lawrenceville, Georgia
https://www.familysafeshelters.com/

ILLINOIS

Southern Illinois Storm Shelters, Inc.
Benton, Illinois
https://www.sheltersonline.com/

Safe Sheds Sales, Inc.
Salem, Illinois
https://www.safesheds.com/

INDIANA

Kentuckiana Storm Shelters
Palmyra, Indiana
https://www.lifelongshelters.com/

Nix Storm Shelters
Poseyville, Indiana
http://www.nixstormshelters.com/

IOWA

Storm Shelters of Iowa
Clive, Iowa
http://stormsheltersofia.com/

Fairfield Precast Concrete
Fairfield, Iowa
https://www.fairfieldprecastconcrete.com/

KANSAS

Drop Zone Storm Shelters
Burden, Kansas
http://dropzoneshelters.com/

Protection Shelters, LLC
Wichita, Kansas
https://protectionshelters.com/

KENTUCKY

Midsouth Storm Shelters
Russellville, Kentucky
https://midsouthshelters.com/

Kentucky Storm Shelters, LLC
Campbellsville, Kentucky
http://kentuckystormshelters.com/

MAINE

Northeast Bunkers
http://northeastbunkers.com/

MICHIGAN

Michigan Storm Shelter, LLC
Westland, Michigan
https://michiganstormshelter.com/

MINNESOTA

PRA Construction Services
https://praservices.com/

Crest Precast Concrete
La Crescent, Minnesota
http://crestprecastconcrete.com/

MISSISSIPPI

Supercell Shelters of Tupelo, LLC
Belden, Mississippi
http://supercellshelters.com/

Bost Tornado Shelters
Pontotoc, Mississippi
http://bosttornadoshelters.com/

MISSOURI

FamilySafe Certified Storm Shelters & Saferooms
Republic, Missouri
https://www.familysafemo.com/

Red Zone Storm Shelters
Springfield, Missouri
http://redzonestormshelters.com/

OKLAHOMA

Oklahoma Shelters
Oklahoma City, Oklahoma
https://www.oklahomashelters.net/

Storm Safe Shelters
Oklahoma City, Oklahoma
https://stormsafeshelters.com/

SOUTH DAKOTA

Divine Concrete, Inc.
Bonesteel, South Dakota
http://www.divineconcrete.com/

TENNESSEE

Fain Storm Shelters
Jackson, Tennessee
https://fainstormshelters.com/

Steel Storm Shelters, LLC
Henderson, Tennessee
https://www.steelstormshelters.com/

TEXAS

Texas Storm Shelter
Plano, Texas
https://www.texasstormshelter.com/

Jarrell Storm Shelters
Jarrell, Texas
http://jarrellstormshelters.com/

VIRGINIA

Nansemond Pre-Cast Concrete, Co.
Suffolk, Virginia
http://www.nansemondprecast.com/

NATIONWIDE STORM SHELTER DEALERS

GRAINGER

https://www.grainger.com/search?searchBar=true&searchQuery=storm+shelters&optOut=0

LOWE'S HOME IMPROVEMENT

https://www.lowes.com/search?searchTerm=storm+shelter

HOME DEPOT

https://www.homedepot.com/s/storm%2520shelter?NCNI-5

TRACTOR SUPPLY COMPANY

https://www.tractorsupply.com/tsc/search/storm%20shelter

U.S. SAFE ROOM

https://www.ussaferoom.com/products/

IN-GROUND GARAGE STORM SHELTERS

GROUND ZERO STORM SHELTERS

https://www.groundzeroshelters.com/underground-garage-shelters

TORNADO TOUGH TORNADO SHELTERS

https://tornadotoughshelters.com/storm-shelters/under-garage#show

EMERGENCY LOCATING DEVICE SELECTION INFO

https://www.rei.com/learn/expert-advice/personal-locator-beacons.html

IN-HOME SAFE ROOM/PANIC ROOM DEALERS

ULTIMATE BUNKER

https://ultimatebunker.com/safe-rooms/

THE PANIC ROOM COMPANY

https://thepanicroomcompany.com/

PANIC ROOM BUILDERS

http://panicroombuilders.com/

SAFEROOM

https://saferoom.com/

VAULT DOOR DEALERS

SAFE AND VAULT STORE

https://www.safeandvaultstore.com/collections/vault-doors-for-panic-rooms-walk-in-safes

SMITH SECURITY SAFES

https://www.smithsecuritysafes.com/vault-doors

CHAMPION SAFE

https://championsafe.com/vault-doors/

LIBERTY SAFE

https://www.libertysafe.com/safe-vault-door-safes-ps-13.html

VAULT PRO USA

https://www.vaultprousa.com/vault-doors

ELECTRONIC ACCESS LOCK INFORMATION

https://www.top5reviewed.com/biometric-fingerprint-door-lock/

https://www.gokeyless.com/blog/what-you-need-to-know-about-fingerprint-locks/

https://www.lowes.com/pd/Barska-Black-Biometric-Lock/1000582749

https://www.homedepot.com/b/Hardware-Door-Hardware-Door-Locks-Electronic-Door-Locks/Biometric/N-5yc1vZc2bdZ1z1brrs

WEATHER RADIOS

http://bestreviews.com/best-weather-radios

https://midlandusa.com/product-category/weather/

https://weatherstationexpert.com/best-weather-radio-reviews/

https://www.weather.gov/mob/nwrhelp

FEMA SAFE ROOM FUNDING

https://www.fema.gov/safe-room-funding

https://www.sapling.com/5744318/federal-assistance-storm-shelter

http://nssa.cc/home/residential-safe-room/financing-rebate-programs/

FEMA STORM SHELTER GUIDE P-320

https://www.fema.gov/fema-p-320-taking-shelter-storm-building-safe-room-your-home-or-small-business

https://www.fema.gov/media-library/assets/documents/2009?id=1536

HOME EMERGENCY KITS TO KEEP IN YOUR SHELTER

READY.GOV

https://www.ready.gov
https://www.ready.gov/kit
https://www.ready.gov/resources

RED CROSS

https://www.redcross.org/store/preparedness

CDC

https://www.cdc.gov/disasters/index.html

COMMUNITY EMERGENCY RESPONSE TEAM (C.E.R.T.)

https://www.ready.gov/cert

EMERGENCY SUPPLY WEBSITES

CAROLINA READINESS

https://carolinareadiness.com/

TENNESSEE READINESS

https://www.tennesseereadiness.com/

EMERGENCY ESSENTIALS

https://www.beprepared.com/survival-and-emergency-kits

BLUE MONSTER PREP

https://bluemonsterprep.com/collections/home-family

THE READY STORE

https://www.thereadystore.com/

HOME EMERGENCY KIT CHECKLIST

____ Water (minimum 1 gallon per person)

____ Emergency Foods (granola bars, beef jerky, etc.)

____ Flashlights or Lanterns (with extra batteries)

____ Emergency Radio

____ Whistle / Air Horn

____ Blankets

____ Cell Phone

____ First Aid Kit

____ Additional Considerations

____ Prescription Medications

____ Copies of Important Papers (digital or paper)

     (Birth Certificates, Insurance and Mortgage, etc)

____ Entertainment Items

     (Playing cards, kid's games, books, etc.)

____ Small Camping Toilet

____ Camp Chairs or Cots

OTHER CONSIDERATIONS

After a natural disaster, there may be dangerous conditions that exist, especially if your home was damaged. Below you will find space to record the locations of critical shut-offs for your home.

Electric Breaker Box _______________________________________

Water Cut-off Valve _______________________________________

Gas Cut-off Valve _______________________________________

Since many people also like to store their valuables in a shelter or safe room, you will find space below to catalog those valuables. This will allow you a checklist to consult should a storm warning occur in your area which will help you to more efficiently move your heirlooms or other valuable items into your storm shelter if they aren't already there.

HEIRLOOM/VALUABLE ITEM INVENTORY

CHOOSING THE RIGHT SHELTER

It's advisable to get multiple quotes when shopping for the right shelter. Here is an area where you can keep track of the various manufacturers and models you are considering and the pricing and specifics on each. Some companies offer financing, so make sure to ask about that as well.

MANUFACTURER

____

MODEL

____

SPECIFICS (SIZE, PRICING, ETC)

____

____

____

____

MANUFACTURER

____

MODEL

____

SPECIFICS (SIZE, PRICING, ETC)

____

____

____

MANUFACTURER

MODEL

SPECIFICS (SIZE, PRICING, ETC)

MANUFACTURER

MODEL

SPECIFICS (SIZE, PRICING, ETC)

PHOTOGRAPH CREDITS

Page 11 - Photographs courtesy of Fain Storm Shelters:
https://fainstormshelters.com/

Page 12 - Photographs courtesy of author's personal collection

Page 14 - Photographs courtesy of Fain Storm Shelters
https://fainstormshelters.com/

Page 15 - Photographs courtesy of Fain Storm Shelters
https://fainstormshelters.com/

Page 16 - Photographs courtesy of Tornado Tough Storm Shelters
https://tornadotoughshelters.com/storm-shelters/

Page 17 - Photographs courtesy of Ultimate Bunker
https://ultimatebunker.com/home/

www.ingramcontent.com/pod-product-compliance
Lightning Source LLC
Chambersburg PA
CBHW040242240726

48664CB00001B/238